KV-577-886

'Yuck Pie'
An original concept by Heather Pindar
© Heather Pindar 2022

Illustrated by Amy Zhing

Published by MAVERICK ARTS PUBLISHING LTD
Studio 11, City Business Centre, 6 Brighton Road,
Horsham, West Sussex, RH13 5BB
© Maverick Arts Publishing Limited February 2022
+44 (0)1403 256941

A CIP catalogue record for this book is available at the British Library.

ISBN 978-1-84886-855-7

www.maverickbooks.co.uk

This book is rated as: Turquoise Band (Guided Reading)

Yuck
Pie

by **Heather Pindar**

illustrated by
Amy Zhing

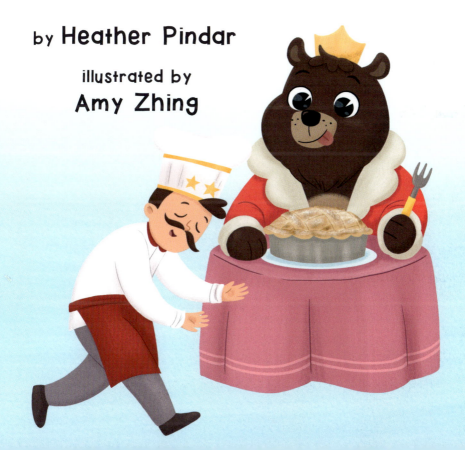

There once was a cook called Snootynose.
He told everybody that he was the best cook
in the whole kingdom.

Every evening at exactly one minute
to six, King Fussytum always shouted,
"Cook Snootynose! I want pie! Bring me pie."

"Here you are, Your Majesty!" Cook Snootynose always said. "Lovely pie, made with only the very best ingredients. And how does it taste?"

Each time, King Fussytum said,

"Oh, it's okay. Not too bad."

Each time, Cook looked upset and said,

"I'm so sorry, King Fussytum.

I will try to do better next time."

Then Cook always went back to the kitchen and crashed his pans about crossly. Kitchen Cat always ran to hide behind the cooker.

Cook Snootynose had three kitchen helpers.

He kept them very busy.

"Crow! Clean
the pots!"
"Yes, Cook!"

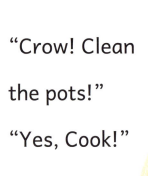

"Frog! Sweep the floor!"

"Yes, Cook!"

"Fox! Write down each ingredient in my big recipe book! My fantastic recipe must not be forgotten."

"Yes, Cook!"

The kitchen helpers were not allowed to cook *anything*, and only Snootynose could wear a SPECIAL HAT.

"If only you worked harder," said Cook to his helpers, "then the king would love all my pies."

The helpers felt sad.

One night, Cook Snootynose was trying out new recipes until the sun came up.

In the afternoon, he was so tired that he fell fast asleep.

At four o'clock Fox said, "Why don't we make the king's pie ourselves? Let's fetch some of our favourite foods to put in it!"

Crow was the first to come back.

"Here's something special for the king's pie.

Delicious worms and red beetles! Mmmm,

yum yum!" Crow fried them in the pan.

Next, Frog hopped back into the kitchen.

"Here's something special for the king's pie.

Delicious slugs! Mmmm, yum yum!"

Frog made the slugs into a sticky slime glaze

for her pastry.

Later, Fox hurried back.

"Here's something special for the king's pie!

Delicious dandelion leaves and stinging nettles!

Mmmm, yum yum!"

Fox boiled them with some old bones to make a

dark green gravy for the pie.

Fox carefully wrote the ingredients in Cook's big recipe book.

At one minute to six, Cook Snootynose woke up.

"King Fussytum's pie! Oh no!" he said. "Relax," said Kitchen Cat, "the helpers made a pie. They're taking it to King Fussytum now."

"Which recipe did they use?" Cook looked in the book. "WHAT!? Worms? Beetles? Slugs? Dandelions? Stinging nettles? NOOOOOOOOOO!"

The clock said six o'clock.

Cook ran up the stairs to the king's dining room,

just in time...

...to see the king take his first mouthful of pie.

The king swallowed. His eyes opened wide.

He belched loudly.

"DELICIOUS! SUPERB! *FANTASTIC!*" he cried.

"Cook, this is the best pie you have ever made!"

The kitchen helpers looked at Cook.

Cook looked at the kitchen helpers.

"I didn't make this pie," said Cook at last.

"Crow, Frog and Fox made the pie."

"I see," said the king. "These kitchen helpers

are fantastic! We are lucky to have them.

From now on, they must have special hats

to wear too."

"Now, Cook. You really MUST taste this delicious pie!" said the king.

"Yes, Cook," said Fox, smiling. "You really must taste the pie."

Frog gave Cook a fork. Cook thought about the worms, beetles, slugs, dandelions, and stinging nettles. He gulped. He took a very small piece of pie.

He slowly put it in his mouth. He swallowed.

His eyes opened wide.

Then Cook's face went all crinkly and a funny shade of green. He clutched his tummy and ran from the dining room.

"My, my!" said King Fussytum. "I wonder

what's wrong with Cook? Now tell me,

what is in this delicious pie?"

"Only the very best ingredients!" said

the kitchen helpers.

From that day on, Cook Snootynose always let Crow, Frog and Fox help with the cooking... and wear special hats of course.

Frog and Crow showed Cook Snootynose where to find delicious wild foods in the garden. Fox taught him how to make her special dark green gravy. And Cook Snootynose even told his helpers how to make the king's favourite chocolate pudding.

And they all cooked happily ever after.

Quiz

1. How many kitchen helpers does Cook Snootynose have?
a) Two
b) Three
c) Five

2. What did Crow bring for the pie?
a) Green beetles and leaves
b) Snails and beetroot
c) Worms and red beetles

3. What did Frog bring for the pie?
a) Slime
b) Slugs
c) Ants

4. What did Fox bring for the pie?

a) Dandelion leaves and stinging nettles

b) Clovers and daffodils

c) Buttercups and daisies

5. What do the kitchen helpers get to wear at the end of the story?

a) Cool aprons

b) Great gloves

c) Special hats

Turn over for answers

Book Bands for Guided Reading

The Institute of Education book banding system is a scale of colours that reflects the various levels of reading difficulty. The bands are assigned by taking into account the content, the language style, the layout and phonics. Word, phrase and sentence level work is also taken into consideration.

Maverick Early Readers are a bright, attractive range of books covering the pink to white bands. All of these books have been book banded for guided reading to the industry standard and edited by a leading educational consultant.

Pink
Red
Yellow
Blue
Green
Orange
Turquoise
Purple
Gold
White

To view the whole Maverick Readers scheme, visit our website at
www.maverickearlyreaders.com

Or scan the QR code above to view our scheme instantly!

Quiz Answers: 1b, 2c, 3b, 4a, 5c